CHADWICK'$ COLLEGE CHECKLI$T

How to Cut College Cost

Charles Adam Chadwick, Jr.

CHADWICK'$ COLLEGE CHECKLI$T

Copyright 2020 by Charles A. Chadwick

Library of Congress Control Number: 2020915026

Chadwick, Charles A.

Correspondence to the author should be directed to:

E-mail: collegechecklist1@gmail.com

All rights are reserved. No part of this publication may be reproduced, distributed, or transmitted in any form or by any means, including photocopying, recording, or any other electronic or mechanical methods, or by any informational storage and retrieval system, without the prior written permission of the Author or Publisher, except in the case of brief quotations embodied in critical reviews and certain other noncommercial uses permitted by copyright law.

ISBN: *978-1-7325697-3-7*

Table of Contents

Page No.

Foreword -- 6
Introduction -- 8

Step 1 Compare Community College vs University Cost -------------- 13

- Escape two simple expenses
- What is gained in two years?
- Examine Transferable credits

Step 2 Student Sacrifice Time --- 23

- What opportunities are on campus?
- How to live on Campus for free
- Take advantage of Summer Breaks

Conclusion -- 36

- Be in control of your education financially tackle any barriers and avoid becoming an asset!

Works Cited -- 46
Acknowledgements -- 47
About The Author -- 49

Legal Disclaimer

The publisher and the author make no guarantees concerning the level of success you may experience by following the advice and strategies contained in this book, and you accept the risk that results will differ for each individual. The author's accounts of examples provided in this book show exceptional results, which may not apply to the average reader, and are not intended to represent or guarantee that you will achieve the same or similar results. Any source of information that was cited is for information purpose only. No source cited is associated by any means with the author's views or reflections.

Foreword

The character and nature of post-secondary education and training is a rapidly evolving process that is being fueled, in large part, by such factors as globalization, science and technology, and social changes. The confluence of these factors, plus many more, is demanding that individuals who expect to become and remain personally and professionally competitive and relevant in the workplace acquire more education and training at ever-increasing levels and rates. Concurrent with the increasing demand for education and training typically is the increase in costs. This trend has persisted for some time and has put the cost of education and training out of reach for many people who have not explored other options for acquiring the knowledge and skills they need without assuming mountains of debt or going broke.

Chadwick'$ College Checkli$t is a small publication that carries a big punch explaining how to minimize the costs of acquiring education and training. Author Charles Adam Chadwick shares some of his personal experiences navigating the financial tricks and traps students often encounter while earning degrees and paying money that is both unnecessary and that they do not have. Many of them, or their parents, often take on enormous debt that can take many years to repay, or they give up altogether on the education and training they desperately need for personal satisfaction and professional growth and development. Either way, there are lost opportunities and financial challenges from which recovery is nearly impossible.

Chadwick did not realize exactly how he had accomplished what seemed like an impossible feat at the time until after he had earned two degrees from two different learning institutions and reflected on how he had done it. By not receiving the financial support from his parents that he had expected to receive, he was forced to figure out how he was going to acquire the education and training he was determined to get. *Chadwick'$ College Checkli$t* details how he did it, and it also gives step-by-step instructions and guidance that others can follow.

His journey through the funding process of his college education is informative and insightful, as well as entertaining in some ways. It is a booklet that will give you a good grounding in how to obtain the education and training you want while maintaining some semblance of financial solvency and greater peace of mind.

INTRODUCTION

This short booklet shares my experience paying for my college education without any prior planning. I cannot promise you anything, but I encourage you to ponder this one statement: "Paying for College can be challenging!" I have two degrees: an associate degree in Electronic Servicing and a bachelor's degree in Mass Media Communications. The associate degree cost me about $3,500, paid all in cash over a (2-year span), and my bachelor's degree cost me $18,200 in student loans over a (3-year span).

My bachelor's degree could have cost me more. An **ADDITIONAL $13,435.96** could have been added the $18,200 in student loans. Had I not figured out how to cut costs, I would have had to add this expense to the existing $18,200.00, all in loans, which could have totaled **$31,635.96.** I am very thankful I did not have that additional cost. I will explain how I reduced my $13,435.96 cost. In this booklet, I will show you that it is possible to cut your costs, and how I showed someone else to reduce their college cost as well.

Before attending college, I successfully graduated from Southwest Onslow High School, home of the "Stallions," in Jacksonville, North Carolina, in May 2003. I did not even want to walk across the stage to accept my high school diploma. Most of my family, on both my mother and father's side, grew up in a farming environment in Jacksonville, North Carolina, so my extended family was huge, full of numerous cousins. From 1991 to about 2015, there had been multiple high school or college graduations among many of my cousins. I had attended so many of them that I was not excited when it was finally my turn, but I did march with my class, more for my mother than for myself.

While I was in high school during my senior year, I made up my mind that after I graduated, I would never pick up a book again or take any more classes. My perspective would change after one year of just working. While taking one year off after graduating and living with my parents, I concluded that I was not happy. In 2004, to improve myself and give me a great sense of achievement and personal satisfaction, I enrolled in my local community college to pursue an associate degree. I discovered that learning, after all, was challenging, but exciting and interesting, nothing like I experienced while in high school. I actually developed a yearning for learning!

I earned my associate degree in the summer of 2006 from Coastal Carolina Community College in my hometown of Jacksonville, NC, and I looked forward to transferring to a university to pursue my bachelor's degree. I applied and was accepted to Lees McRae College, home of the "Bobcats," in Banner Elk, North Carolina, for the 2007 fall semester.

I received my letter of acceptance, along with my financial aid award package. After all grants and scholarships were applied, I had an estimated balance of $3500 remaining for my tuition for the Fall 2007. I was offered a loan to make up the difference. I thought, no problem; I will just ask my father to co-sign the loan for me. When I asked him to co-sign the loan, I was shocked by what happened next!

My father started to sign the loan letter, but he then thought, stopped, and did not co-sign for me. My father informed me that I should have already had my own credit established by then. Please keep in mind that I was still living with my parents so in one sense, my father was right. But, at the same time, my father had never taught me anything about establishing credit either. I was a country boy from North Carolina; all I was ever taught to do in life to get by or to be successful was to believe in God, pray, work hard, and everything would be all right. No one had ever shown me or taught me about credit or finances, so I had no advice or guidance whatsoever on anything related to money. At that moment, I was upset with my father. I could not understand his motive. But now that I have graduated with two degrees, worked, and traveled around the world, I understand what he was trying to teach me. My father wanted me to become independent and develop into a man. This motivated me to sit down and think long and hard about what I had to do. So, I called the financial aid director and asked for a loan without a co-signer, and it was granted.

I know paying for college can be challenging for anyone who has not walked down this path. With today's economy and current financial challenges for many people, I feel like anyone who attends college should avoid or limit student cost as much as possible.

When a student graduates with an education, they may already have debt or some overhead cost from the start of the race to secure wealth for themselves. In 2015, while working as an Armed Guard contractor in the country of Kosovo, I got inspired to write and keep a life journal while following a motivational speaker named Jim Rohn. While working one night on the night shift, I thought about how I was able to reduce my education costs and decided to write how I did it. The information I will share is not about how to **SAVE money.** There is a difference between the words save and cost.

During my time in South Korea in 2019, a co-worker named Glenn explained the difference. Glenn said, *"Charles, if I went to Lowe's to purchase a Washing Machine that retailed for $400, but I purchased it on sale for $300, some people will say that I saved $100, wouldn't they?"* I replied, "Yes, I agree." Glenn continued to say, *"Unless I can put that $100 in my bank account, then I didn't save anything, but what I did do is cut my cost."*

To understand how to cut cost, I would first like to define the word cost. The online Merriam-Webster's Dictionary defines the word **COST.**

a: *the amount or equivalent paid or charged for something:*

b: *the outlay or expenditure (as of effort or sacrifice) made to achieve an object*

SOURCE: "Cost" Merriam-Webster, Merriam-Webster, www.merriam-webster.com/dictionary/cost.

Now that I have defined the word cost, I will cover 2 Steps with sub-pointers that may help one cut cost and limit college debt. I will start with Step 1, followed by Step 2, and conclude with some learning points.

STEP 1

Compare Community College Versus University Costs

During an *"Introduction to Philosophy"* class at my local community college, I remember the professor making a statement that still sticks with me: *"In this class, it's not my job to teach you WHAT to think but HOW to think."* If you can adopt this mentality while reading this booklet, I believe it will serve you well throughout your life. **Again, I am not perfect, nor do I claim to be an expert. But, if anything, I just want to share information on what can be done to cut college education cost.**

As mentioned earlier, I have an associate degree that cost me about $3,500.00. Had I attended a four-year university for those first two years, my expense undoubtedly would have been much more. The reason I say this is because other expenses can occur while attending a four-year college or university. For example, my room fee was an expense that I had to pay for the first-year semester while attending university, but I did not have these expenses while attending community college for two years because I was living with my parents.

At a university, one may be charged for a campus dorm room while attending all four years. By starting out at the local community college, I escaped two expenses for two years. I lived with my parents rent-free during that time. Now, if I were not working towards a degree and doing something positive with my life, there was no way my parents would have allowed me to stay rent-free. We had an agreement, which was two years of not having to pay any room fees as long as I was in school. I know you are wondering about the price difference. Well, at the time I transferred to a university in the fall of 2007 to pursue my bachelor's degree, my college room fee average was close to $3,500 for Fall and Spring semesters. Had I attended the first two years at the university at the rate of $3,500 per year, I would have paid $7,000 for two years of college ($3,500 multiplied by 2 years), which does not include tuition, meal plans, books, parking fee and other college expenses.

Let us compare $7,000 for two years of college at a university just for living expenses with $3,500 and the completion of an associate degree. I have an important question to ask about paying for college expenses: As a student, would you be willing to take out a loan just for a room fee of $7,000, or pay $3,500 over two-years and you would have received an associate degree? I really want you to focus on the idea of an associate degree, which I will address later. The next expense I will address is the meal plan, which I also avoided by attending a community college for the first two years. When I transferred to the university, I was required to purchase a meal plan while I stayed on camp us, even though I never used what I pre-paid for in the meal plan. I never consistently ate three meals a day, seven days a week. In an online article by Melissa Burns titled "Ways to Save Money on Food in College," she states:

"If you're required to purchase a meal plan, choose the right one. It can be tricky, but it's ridiculous to pay for three meals a day if you're not likely to eat them all. Money Magazine reports that students who eat every meal on campus spend around 85 percent more each day than students who cook at home. Decide how you'll use the plan. For example, if you like a big breakfast but prefer to eat light meals for the rest of the day, buy the plan with the fewest meals. Enjoy breakfast each morning at school but prepare everything else at home. If, on the other hand, you don't trust yourself to stay out of restaurants, go all out for the plan with the most meals."

SOURCE:
Burns, Melissa. "The College Puzzle A College Success Blog by Dr. Michael W Kirst." The College Puzzle, 20 May 2017, collegepuzzle.stanford.edu/7-ways-to-save-money-on-food-in-college/

In my opinion, some meals will be missed, depending on your own class schedule and how you manage your time. Now, here are some other important questions for students and parents: In your everyday life when you grocery shop, do you buy groceries for a year, six months, or every two weeks? Would you be willing to take out a loan when paying for college expenses such as the meal plan? What if you could look at other options? Maybe pay monthly or weekly cash to your child for their food expenses and keep that cost down?

Now, I understand that a student must eat; it is essential to everyday living, but to take out a LOAN to finance that expense should be eliminated if possible. Again, the meal plan is just the food aspect, not the actual education part of college. I wonder how many students have taken out a loan to maybe pay for a meal plan while in college. Could this situation possibility exist? A student who has graduated is no longer eating on campus, but they are still paying back a loan. If students looked at other options, then they might be able to cut costs and avoid a loan.

In an online article titled *"Dining Costs Eating up College Students' Budget,"* author Bill Fay stated something interesting:

"As the cost of college skyrockets, students are searching for ways to cut expenses. A good place to look is on their dinner plates. Food expenses can wreck a budget if a busy student eats out regularly. What might surprise you is how much a

student spends eating in. By eating in, we mean using the meal plans colleges offer at campus dining halls. Unfortunately, "offer" is not quite accurate. Most colleges require students to sign up for meal plans at some point in their time on campus. The fact is a lot of schools are getting fat on those plans. The best way to keep food costs from sending you deeper into debt is to prepare your own meals as often as possible."

Fay, Bill. "Dining Costs Eating up College Students' Budget." *Debt.Org,* 9 Mar. 2018, www.debt.org/blog/dining-costs-eating-up-college-students-budget.

At the end of each semester, I would always have some meals left on my account balance, but I could not cash them out. At the end of the day, I basically paid for something that I did not fully use. In other words, I could not get a refund for the meals I pre-purchased but did not eat, regardless of the reasons. Always look at the best option for a meal plan and explore numerous options that may cut cost.

Now that I have covered the cost of room fees and the meal plan that can be avoided by attending a community college for the first two years, let me share with you a scenario of cost comparison. Let us say a student was accepted to a university and, after financial aid was awarded, the student is short $10,000. Would it be beneficial for the student to take out a loan for $10,000 right from the start? Keep in mind this is the first year of college, and a student is already starting out with a debt of $10,000. In addition, the student has three more years to finish his or her bachelor's degree. In a community college, I believe one can cut costs and maybe avoid taking out a loan. Remember, earlier in the introduction of this book, I stated that my associate degree only cost me an estimated $3,500 over two years versus four years.

In one year, a student could easily accumulate a $10,000 debt, for example, for one year of college at a university with no degree versus $3,500 for two years of community college and obtain an associate degree. Therefore, there are reasons to explore the **"DEAL"** by starting out at a community college first. Are you ready? Credits sometimes earned from a community college can be transferred to a four-year university. I know this can happen because I did it! When I completed my associate degree in Electronic Servicing back in 2006, I was able to transfer some credits to Lees McRae College, which allowed me to enter the university as a first- semester sophomore.

From BIG FUTURE, a College Board on-line article titled "Tips on Transferring from a 2-Year to a 4-Year College," there is a passage that explains the process of how to transfer. The passage states, "So what happens when you transfer? Your four-year college will look at the courses you took and the grades you earned at your two-year college and decide how much credit to give you. Each course is worth a certain number of credits, often three, and students need to earn enough credits, usually, 120, to graduate.

SOURCE: Handel, Stephen. "Tips on Transferring from a 2-Year to a 4-Year College." *Tips on Transferring from a 2-Year to a 4-Year College,*bigfuture.collegeboard.org/find-colleges/college-101/tips-on-college-transferring-from-a-2-year-to-a-4-year-college.

This is what could happen to a student who plans on transferring. Again, after all my credits were evaluated and considered, I was able to start as a first-semester sophomore. Please keep in mind that my associate degree in Electronics Servicing was not in the same field as my Mass Media Communication Bachelor's degree. Many of my elective classes were transferable because they were mainly core classes or, in other words, generic classes.

Again, my associate degree cost me about $3,500 cash, and had I attended a four-year university for my first two years, I may have started out in debt. What do you think? Another interesting fact about some community colleges is that they have payment plans. I did not have to pay the $3,500 for my associate degree all at once. I took advantage of the community college's Deferred Payment Plan. Instead of paying my college bill for a semester or quarter all at once, I was able to pay in monthly installments. The balance had to be paid off completely by the end of my academic period, and I had to also maintain a certain GPA during this time. By participating in this plan, I was able to work and pay as I go. I would like to thank a gentleman working in the admissions department when I was registering at Coastal Carolina Community College who suggested that I consider the deferred plan. Had he not informed me of this payment option, I do not think I would have even attended college, because I did not have the upfront, out-of-pocket money for the entire academic year.

As a student, I want you to know that you will have options for the first couple of years of your college education. What I find interesting is that sometimes students do not know that they can, or they are unwilling or refuse to change their major. I witnessed some classmates who remained in majors that did not suit them or in which they could not excel. How often will students change their major?

This article dates to October 12, 2018, posted by Linda Larsen titled, 'NCES (National Center Education Statistics) report: About 80 percent of college students change their major at least once.' In the opening passage of this article, the second paragraph reads " Trying to figure out what you are going to do for the rest of your life during your first year of college can be a daunting task, so at Idaho State University this week, advisors are doing everything they can to help in those decisions." This passage confirms what I have seen; sometimes, students do not know right from the start what career field they will choose or have a real interest in. Towards the end of the same online article, the NCES gives the percentage of how many students changes major. "According to the National

Center for Education Statistics, about 80 percent of college students change their major at least once. Nationally, many students change their majors as many as six times before they decide on a career. Advisors hope that career weeks like this will help reduce that number."

SOURCE: Larsen, Linda. "NCES Report: About 80 Percent of College Students Change Major At least Once." *KIFI,* KIFI, 13 Oct. 2018, www.localnews8.com/news/education/nces-report-about-80-percent-of-college-students-change-major-at-least-once/806483499.

If a person does not know what they would like to major in, why would they pay thousands of dollars to a university while their personal and professional needs are not being met? Instead, they could attend a community college for two years and take some classes that would cost less and that could be transferred. This is just an option that worked for me, and it may work for you also, depending on your circumstances.

For the record, I did not know beforehand that some of my credits earned from my community college would, indeed, transfer to a university, but now you are conscious of this. If you want to know if a certain class credit will transfer, just write down the classes you have taken from a community college and ask the admissions department of the university you want to attend if those classes will transfer. Another thing you can do is to ask the admissions office at the university you want to transfer to if they will transfer credits from a class you want to take at the community college *before* you take the class.

Below is a screenshot of some of my community college credits that were transferred from Coastal Carolina Community College and accepted by Lees McRae. The interesting thing about this screenshot is that all the listed courses that transferred were not all completed while I was pursuing my associate degree. Three of the courses were completed after my first year of transferring to the university. In the summer break of 2008 while home, I returned to my local community college with a specific objective mind, which I will explain later. Can you guess why I would go back to my local community college after I had completed one year at the university? Next is STEP 2 of my checklist. How badly does a student want to cut college cost, and what are they willing to sacrifice?

Course		Title	Grd R	Hrs Att	Hrs Capt	Grade Points	Course Dates
LIT	230	American Literatur	P	0.00	3.00	0.00000	08/01/08-08/01/08
PRD	115	Fitness for Life	P	0.00	3.00	0.00000	08/01/08-08/01/08
PHI	224	Intro. to Philosop	P	0.00	3.00	0.00000	08/01/08-08/01/08
CIS	104	Intro to Comp & Ap	P	0.00	3.00	0.00000	01/01/91-01/01/91
RHE	101	Rhetoric I	P	0.00	3.00	0.00000	01/01/91-01/01/91
ENG	188	Sp Tp in English	P	0.00	3.00	0.00000	01/01/91-01/01/91
MAT	112	College Algebra	P	0.00	3.00	0.00000	01/01/91-01/01/91
PSY	233	Genoral Psychology	P	0.00	3.00	0.00000	01/01/91-01/01/91
REL	288	Special Topics	P	0.00	3.00	0.00000	01/01/91-01/01/91
		Non Term Totals:		0.00	26.00	0.0000 GPA =	0.0000
		Cumulative Totals:		0.00	26.00	0.0000 GPA =	0.0000

STEP 2

Student Sacrifice Time

Former United States President, John F. Kennedy, once said, *"Ask Not What Your Country Can Do for You; Ask What You Can Do for Your Country."* As a student, paying for college is a responsibility, but make sure you are willing to help on the cost as well! Do not depend on your parents or someone else. There are so many ways to cut costs when a student takes advantage of opportunities while attending college. For example, I qualified for a federal program while I was in college.

The Federal Work-Study program allows a student with a financial need to work on campus part-time jobs for undergraduate and graduate students with financial need, allowing them to earn money to help pay education expenses. The program encourages community service work and work related to the student's course of study.

SOURCE : https://studentaid.ed.gov/sa/types/work-study.

I took advantage of this program and earned extra money to help pay for my college expenses. The Work-Study program could sometimes be the difference between paying money out-of-pocket or taking out a loan for college expenses. Worked two jobs on campus with the Federal Work-Study Program. I worked with the Maintenance Department on campus, and I had the chance to work with the IT-Tech Services repairing computers. I would like to personally thank the IT Director at the time for Lees McRae College for giving me many invaluable learning experiences in the IT world. My job duties included troubleshooting hardware/software issues, registering new students' MAC address to the college network, and performing service calls throughout the campus. I would work the maximum number of hours allowable every semester. Once my college expenses were paid in full, I could use the balance of what I earned, if any, for my personal use.

Below are two pictures of me while working with the Maintenance Department on campus. One is of me checking for a pipe leak, and the other is of me shoveling snow off a stairway in front of a college dorm. I would work early before my classes 7am - 9am and after my classes finished 3pm - 5pm. I recall some students laughing at me working because they had too much pride to be seen with a weed eater trimming grass around the college campus, but I was not ashamed. What many students did not know was that usually at the end of the semester, I would get a refund check. After the expense of my owed account balance was paid off each semester, I would keep the extra money for myself. This is how I paid other college expenses and had extra money for miscellaneous things.

 In the introduction, I stated that my bachelor's degree cost me about $18,200 in student loans, but an additional $13,435.96 could have been added to that amount. Had I not cut costs by participating in the federal work-study program, I would have had to add $4,610.96 to the existing $18,200 (loans). That $4610.96 I earned was part of the $13,435.96 for which I did not have to take out a loan to cover my college education expenses. Do the math: $13,434.96, minus $4610.96 (Work Study) equals $8,825. Please remember this figure $ 8,825. I will explain next where this cost was eliminated.

Another opportunity I took advantage of that reduced my costs was becoming a Resident Assistant (RA). A Resident Assistant is someone who lives in the dorm to help enforce the rules, mediate disagreements, and provide general community support for other students. In other words, the job description of an RA is to be a mentor within the dormitory and on the campus. The only thing I had to do to become an RA was to apply for the position, so I did and got the job. I would have never thought to apply for this position or a responsibility like this, but I was encouraged to do so.

A Mr. Justin Kitts, who was my RA then, but now the current Dean of Students at Lees McRae College as of June 18, 2019, had recruited me for the 2008 spring semester. He pulled me aside one day and said, *""I think you should apply for the upcoming RA position; you would be a good fit."* At first, I was not sold on going for the position. He continued, *"Charles, some of the perks of being an RA is that you get a room by yourself, your room fee would get waived, and you can put this title on your resume, which will look good later on in your life."* I still was not sold, but I took the challenge and applied. I went through an interview and competed with other students through a board-selection process. I made all the cuts and was selected.

The position was challenging at times, but I did not find it unusually difficult. All I had to do was occasionally stay on campus in my dorm building and be on watch duty sometimes. Another part of the job was to conduct room inspections, check fire extinguishers and respond to fire or trouble alarms throughout my building. For duty watch at the rate of one weekend out of each month, I would sit in the front lobby, checking student ID cards and making rounds throughout the dormitory building. I remember my dorm was an all-freshman boy's facility called "Tennessee Residence Hall." Sometimes there were some issues, but I always had floor meetings and resolved most of the problems.

My room fee was waived, just for becoming an RA and volunteering my time. I would come back each summer about a week early to prepare for new students arriving and being on duty watch one weekend out the month. In other words, I was able to live in the dorm FREE. I held my position as an RA for two and a half years. Had I not been an RA, my room fee would have been an estimated $3,500 per year, and I would have needed to take out a loan to cover my room expense. Calculated what my bill would have been approximately $3,500 per year for 2.5 years, (2.5 years multiplied by $3500); the total cost would have been $8,750!

In an online article from the Sallie Mae website titled "How becoming an RA changed my life and helped me pay for college" author Bryana Blanco shared her tuition expense while she was NOT a Resident Assistant versus after becoming one. Ms. Blanco stated,

"For her first year of college, she was charged around $10,000 per semester, about $20,000 for the year, which includes her meal plan, rent, credits taken, books, and other university fees. For her second year, she lived in the same location and signed up for the same meal plan, but it was compensated by the RA position. Her tuition per semester then became around $7,000, totaling to around $14,000 for the year with the same amount of credits and fees/charges considered. She saved a little over $6,000 through this position without having to change her lifestyle or classes and without having to leave campus! This position can be held for three years, meaning she could save about $18,000 while receiving her bachelors; that is almost a full year of school paid completely. The savings add up and can allow you to invest in other important factors in your life, like a car, graduate school, travel plans, and so much more. The possibilities are endless."

SOURCE:
Blanco, Bryana. "How Becoming an RA Changed My Life and Helped Me Pay for College." Sallie Mae, 26 Sept 2018, www.salliemae.com/blog/becoming-resident-assistant-helped-pay-for-college/

I want you to know that while paying for your own college education, try to make sure you always look at different ways to **CUT COSTS** in the process. On the next page is a screenshot of my college credits, scholarships, and loans from Fall 2007 through Spring 2010 semesters. Please look at the circled blocks that show my Federal Work-Study earned amounts *($4610.96)* and my RA room waiver amounts *($8825)*.

2007/FALL and 2008/SPRING

Award	Description	Amount	Act	Date
LMCIG	Burton Scholarship	3,000.00	A	07/16/07
NCLTG	NC Legislative Tuitio	1,950.00	A	08/07/07
PELL	Federal Pell Grant	660.00	A	07/16/07
SCSF	NC State Contractual	1,000.00	A	07/16/07

Award	Description	Amount	Act	Date
FWS	Federal Work Study	1,600.00	A	07/16/07
STAFS	Direct Loan - Subsidi	3,500.00	A	08/17/07
NCELS	NC Educational Lotter	1,840.00	A	08/22/07

Parents "rejected" the parent loan.

Room Waiver was for sping semester only.

Award	Description	Amount	Act	Date
PLUS	Direct Loan - PLUS	4,700.00	R	07/26/07
GLADE	Glade Valley Scholars	2,500.00	A	09/04/07
CROUS	Crouse Family Scholar	5,300.00	A	09/20/07
RAROO	RA Room Waiver	1,625.00	*	12/10/07

Room Waiver was for sping semester only.

2008/FALL and 2009/SPRING

Award	Description	Amount	Act	Date
RAROO	RA Room Waiver	3,500.00	A	06/04/08
NCLTG	NC Legislative Tuitio	1,950.00	A	06/04/08
LMCIG	Burton Scholarship	500.00	A	09/15/08
CROUS	Crouse Family Scholar	5,784.00	A	09/15/08
PELL	Federal Pell Grant	4,731.00	A	07/09/08

Award	Description	Amount	Act	Date
SCSF	NC State Contractual	3,516.00	A	09/15/08
FWS	Federal Work Study	1,386.96	A	07/09/08
STAFS	Direct Loan - Subsidi	4,500.00	A	07/11/08
GLADE	Glade Valley Scholars	2,500.00	A	09/15/08

2009/FALL and 2010/SPRING

Award	Description	Amount	Act	Date
RAROO	RA Room Waiver	3,700.00	A	07/16/09
PELL	Federal Pell Grant	5,350.00	A	07/16/09
NCLTG	NC Legislative Tuitio	1,821.00	A	08/12/09
SCSF	NC State Contractual	3,500.00	A	07/16/09
LMCIG	Burton Scholarship	5,500.00	A	07/16/09

Award	Description	Amount	Act	Date
GLADE	Glade Valley Scholars	2,500.00	A	07/16/09
FWS	Federal Work Study	1,624.00	A	07/16/09
STAFS	Direct Loan - Subsidi	5,500.00	A	07/16/09

Do you remember towards the end of Step 1 when I asked why I would go back to my local community college in the summer of 2008 after one year at the university? This is the answer: Another way I cut costs while attending college was by taking advantage of educational opportunities that could reduce my overall cost. I remember looking at how much one class cost per semester at the university, and I came up with a great idea. The idea was to take some elective classes at the same community college over the summer break that were cheaper and transferable to the university. I also knew that this idea could allow me to graduate early and have an easy senior year before I graduated with my bachelor's degree in Mass Media Communication. I can proudly tell you that I was able to have an easy senior year. My senior year was very relaxing, and for two of my classes, I was a lab assistant in the Apple Mac Lab. Being a Lab Assistant, all I did was open and close the lab all semester for students who were also majoring in Mass Media Communications.

This is how I was successful at executing my plan into action. Before I left my college for the summer break, I met up with my academic advisor to see if my idea would work. My advisor looked over the classes I wanted to take and approved them as transferable. I ended up taking three electives classes: Philosophical Issues, American Literature and Fit/Wellness for life. I took all three classes at the same community college from which I received my associate degree. All three classes were accepted and transferred to the university as credits toward my bachelor's degree and appear on my college transcript.

Just imagine if every summer a college student returns home from the university and takes some classes at their local community college? They may be able to graduate early and cut costs. Even at the high school level, a parent could also help their child get a head start in college by allowing the child to start taking some college courses over the summer at a community college. Just imagine even if a student in high school was to begin taking college classes every summer before they graduated from high school. This can happen in today's world for sure. When I was in high school, I did not hear about this information nor was I guided to start taking college courses early. Where would a student be academically when they start college? After taking college classes every summer, could a high school student enter their first year of college as a second semester freshmen or sophomore? Who knows?

I have talked about how I did cut down my college cost throughout this booklet, but now let me share a story of how I helped a friend named Pamela, pictured here, cut her cost as well. I remember looking over her financial aid award letter. She was transferring to Virginia State University on a partial basketball scholarship. Before transferring to Virginia State as a second-semester sophomore, she had attended Catawba College in Salisbury, North Carolina. By reviewing her awarded financial aid letter, I saw an opportunity where she could get a $4,500.00 refund check.

Here is the good thing about scholarships: in some cases, a student can move off campus and eliminate the room and the meal plan fees. If it is allowed, a student can do exactly that and be refunded the amount for the room fee and meal plan if the scholarship covers all other expenses. This is exactly what I did for my friend. She moved off campus and received a check of $4500.00 at the beginning of each semester. She then took the $4,500.00 refund check and found a room for rent off-campus for $550.00 per month. After her junior year, she found another room off campus for $350.00 a month and was still able to continue getting a refund check from the college.

Future or current students, if you have received a scholarship that covers all college expenses, I would suggest finding a place off campus that is cheaper if that is feasible and beneficial for you. I knew a student who was a basketball player on scholarship who used his refund check money to buy himself a car. Just imagine what you could do when you cut cost and receive a college refund check. Could a refund check help you if you needed a car, an iPad, or even a plane ticket to go home for a visit during the holidays? This brings me to the end of Step 2. Students, make sure you are willing to sacrifice your time and best efforts to meet your goal of cutting cost.

One last thing that is old-fashioned and the American Way is to work hard. Even though I was a college student, I also held a job as a Security Guard off-campus with a company named "The Budd Group." I worked at a high-end, luxury, and gated community called "Headwaters" in the gorgeous Blue Ridge Mountains of Banner Elk, North Carolina. I cannot explain in words how beautifully this community was developed. I am incredibly happy that I had the opportunity and pleasure to work there. I would only work there on the weekends since I was in school as a full-time student. This job allowed me to make extra money while I pursued my degree. Also, after I graduated in May 2010, I was still able to work with the same security company until December 2011 when I accepted another position.

Everyone, please do not sell yourself short in this life. You have a responsibility to provide the best future for yourself, but make sure you learn to sacrifice your time. Below is an actual picture of me working at the gated community, Headwaters.

Conclusion

You have now completed Chadwick's College Checklist. Let us review the 2 Steps with sub-pointers that may help someone minimize their college cost. Remember **Step 1:** *Compare Community College versus University Cost.* Step 1 <u>sub-pointers</u> within the first two years of college try to control meal plan, room fees and examine transferable credits. **Step 2:** *Student Sacrifice Time.* Step 2 <u>sub-pointers</u> investigate all areas such as Federal Work-Study Program, Resident Assistant Position, Summer Classes, and the old fashion way, which is to just work hard. This was my experience on how I personally cut cost of my college education. Everything that I shared I did unintentionally while attending college, but now you can also reduce your college cost intentionally.

In some cases, people may have *planned* how to defray the cost or expense of a college education. Parents, especially, sometimes pay by setting up a 529 Educational Savings Plan or a Personal Savings Account, Custodial Account, Home Equity loan (putting their home up as collateral), or they tap into retirement plans by borrowing money from their 401-K. These are all ways to pay for a college education, but the information I have shared is all based upon a student just making some personal choices that could cut cost.

In my opinion, this is not rocket science, but the idea of a person cutting college cost by having an open mind and being willing to make some personal sacrifices. Now, with any college expense, a scholarship can be a wonderful thing. Scholarships can assist with the cost and expenses but ONLY for the student who receives them.

The next option for a student or parent is to pay out-of-pocket or go into debt by taking out a student loan. If you can afford to pay your own expense, that is one way to go. But, if you cannot afford it, like I couldn't when I was a student, then please think about my next statement. Everyone, please, *"Use all of your resources to limit your college cost!"* Now, I did eliminate some of my college costs, which I covered, but I still had to take out some student loans. I'm now debt free of my student loan balance. I have 100% paid back in full the original $18,200 and any added interest. It felt good to have paid off my loans and move forward with my life.

Loans are not a bad thing when it comes down to a person's education, career, and future. Please view your student loan as an investment. Whenever one can limit their actual college cost, then they may limit or avoid debt. How would a person feel if they are paying back a student loan that they could have possibly reduced or even avoided? How will you now go about reducing your college cost? In May 2019, while working as a contractor in South Korea, I read a book that intrigued me titled, *"FAKE: Fake Money, Fake Teachers, Fake Assets: How Lies Are Making the Poor and Middle-Class Poorer,"* by Robert T. Kiyosaki. Robert is also the well-known author of the famous book titled *"Rich Dad, Poor Dad: What the Rich Teach Their Kids about Money That the Poor and Middle*

Class Do Not!" In his book FAKE, there was a passage that really captured my attention and interest:

"In 2012, student loan debt surpassed the $1 trillion mark, as well as credit card debt. As of 2018, federal student loan debt is the number one asset of the U.S. government. The way I see it, the United States went from subprime mortgages for poor people to subprime education for poor students. Subprime mortgages can be forgiven via bankruptcy. Most subprime education loans can never be forgiven." SOURCE: "Subprime Education." FAKE: Fake Money, Fake Teachers, Fake Assets: How Lies Are Making the Poor and Middle-Class Poorer, by Robert T. Kiyosaki, Plata Publishing, 2019, pp. 153-153.

Do you agree with the passage that the number one asset for our U.S. government is student loan debt? There are 2 key sentences from this passage that intrigued me, and it may also intrigue you, **"the number one asset of the U.S. government is federal student loan debt and that most subprime education loans can never be forgiven."**

Please look at the charts on the next page. The Charts are from an on-line article by Jill Mislinski. Please examine the charts on the next page for information purposes. The on-line article is titled "The Fed's Financial Accounts: What Is Uncle Sam's Largest Asset" by Jill, Mislinski, 06/12/20. Towards the end of the article an interesting statement was made. Jill stated "Student loans may be a liability on the consumer balance sheet, but they constitute an asset for Uncle Sam. Just how big? It's about 44.8 percent of the total Federal assets.

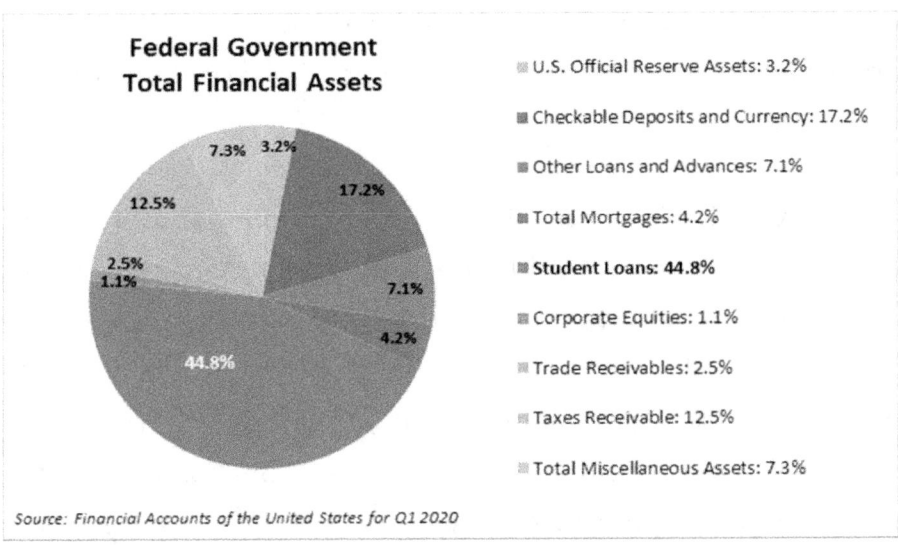

Source: Financial Accounts of the United States for Q1 2020

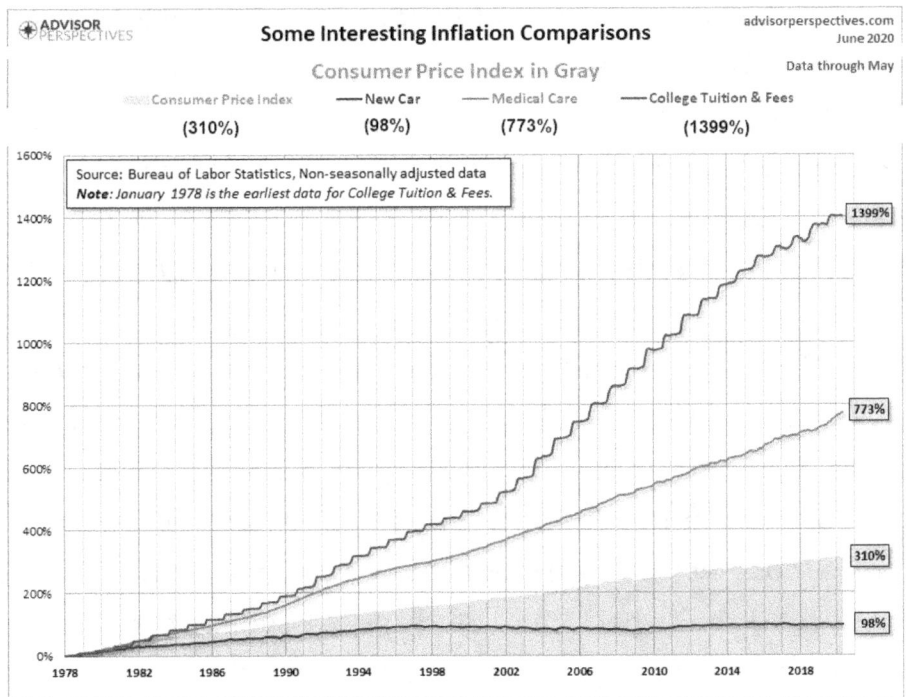

This is 10.8 times larger than the 4.2 percent for the Total Mortgages outstanding and 3.6 times the size of Taxes

Receivable at 12. 5 percent." Please examine the pie chart graph pictured and look at the comparison of all categories in relation to student loans.

From the Pie Chart the biggest section is students loans that account for 44.8% of the Federal Government total assets. Below the Pie Graph is an inflation graph comparison. In the same article Jill continued to reflect on the results from the Inflations Comparison Graph. *"During the decade of the 1990's, when real out-of-pocket funding declined 25%, tuition and fees rose 92%, which sounds substantial ... until you compare it to the 1399% across the complete data series. For early boomers paying for college was sort of like buying a car. But in recent decades, it has become more like buying a house, for which the strategy of a minimum down payment is commonplace for first-time buyers. The student loan bubble, the biggest slice in Uncle Sam's asset pie, will haunt us for many years to come."*

Who has the answers? After viewing the graphs, I have provided do you see just how much students' loans weigh in as an asset? Let me explain something; when a person takes out a loan for a car or house and defaults on the loan the car/house can be repossessed. With student loans when a person defaults on their loan what can be repossessed? There is no hard-physical property, but what can be garnished is a person's future wages. This is my opinion; a young person more than likely will be working a good proportion of their lifetime.

Therefore, I would always advise them to keep their college cost down.

I had a funny uncle who once gave me a funny piece of advice that is true. He said Charles" *You should never walk into a marriage blindfolded."* I feel the same way when it comes to students' loans. **STUDENTS PLEASE DON'T TAKE OUT A STUDENT LOAN BLINDFOLDED!** Just remember any student who received a loan usually would have signed a Master Promissory Note (MPN). An MPN is a legal document in which you promise to repay your loan(s) and any accrued interest and fees to the U.S. Department of Education. It also explains the terms and conditions of your loan(s). I will leave you with some questions to think about. Student loans are indeed an asset for the government and if a student has signed an (MPN) can, should and why should their loan/debt be forgiven? Did anyone force a student into the major they chose to study? Lastly, what other asset would the government use to replace student loans if a bail out was given?

I feel that mankind should at least share information that can help others. This reminds me of a passage I heard when I was younger. I am not a deeply religious person, but I do have deep spiritual leanings. Luke, chapter 11 verse 33 (Aramaic Bible) says, *"No man lights a lamp and sets it in a hidden place or under a bushel but over a lamp stand, that those who enter may see its light."* I hope I have shed some light on how to cut costs while paying for a college education.

Sometimes, this world can appear to be a little challenging economically, even living in a nation like America. One thing about living in America is that there is always an OPPORTUNITY. Opportunities can be given, taken, or even created, but one must seek and look for them. The information I have shared contains a few opportunities that I took advantage of to cut my college cost and expenses while pursuing my degrees.

For the record, I have worked in many professions after high school and even after college. Many of the job areas and fields of specialization was not so much relevant to my Communications Degree, but this is the first time I have attempted to communicate some of my experiences in writing. I have always been a communicator and motivator throughout my life.

This year alone in 2020, we are faced with the COVID-19 Pandemic. What I find interesting is that many people are staying extremely optimistic. A student should stay optimistic as well. They will face choices in paying for their college education with the challenge of inflation and trying not to become an asset by going into debt. Now here is my last word of encouragement and bonus advise for a parent or student. With many people working from home during this pandemic now could be the best time to work and go to school on-line until college campuses reopen. If you are planning to work and go to school than find and work for a company that have a tuition reimbursement program. Tuition reimbursement or tuition assistance is when the employer pays for a pre-determined amount of continuing education credits or college coursework to be applied toward a degree. These programs are intended for employees looking to advance their education as it relates to their current career, offering the chance to increase their industry knowledge and developmental skills. Just ask any company if they have a program and maybe you will cut cost. I know about this program, because I was offered it several times though the companies I have worked for. Unfortunately, at the time these opportunities was offered to me I had already obtained my degrees.

Also, sometimes being a college employee allows a person or even their kids to go to the same institution at a discounted cost. This can also result in a person cutting cost as well for their education. Now that I have informed you of some additional information to cut cost please remember the 2 Steps with the sub pointers from this booklet! Use the checklist sheet I have included on the next page. Everyone, please check off the steps from the list to make sure you are doing everything you can to keep costs down before you go on your own college journey experience.

Sincerely,

Charles A. Chadwick Jr.

"A former college student, but more importantly a friend who has shared with you the reader some steps to add or make your own checklist so you can achieve COLLEGE SUCCESS BY CUTTING COSTS."

CUT COLLEGE COSTS CHEAT CHECK LIST SHEET

(Please check off each sub pointers from the 2STEPS & BONUS to make sure you give yourself or your child the best opportunities to cut college cost).

1. Compare Community College Versus University Cost

- ☐ Avoid room fee and meal plan first two years
- ☐ Check to see if you can set up a deferred payment plan with Community College
- ☐ Research what classes will transfer and how many credits they are worth
- ☐ Confirm with the University you want to transfer to if your credits will transfer beforehand
- ☐ When transferring to University, look at the best way to purchase a meal plan.

2. Step 2 Student Sacrifice Time

- ☐ Take advantage of the Federal Work-study Program
- ☐ Look into becoming a Resident Assistant (RA).
- ☐ On summer break, cut costs by taking more college classes.
- ☐ Work hard find a side job.
- ☐ DID YOU DO EVERYTHING YOU COULD TO CUT YOUR COLLEGE EDUCATION COSTS?

3. Bonus for a Parent or Student

- ☐ Check to see if your current or future employer have a Tuition Reimbursement Program.
- ☐ Lastly, look into becoming a college employee if they offer free tuition, reduced tuition or "no student loans".

WORKS CITED

Blanco, Bryana. "How Becoming an RA Changed My Life and Helped Me Pay for College." *Sallie Mae,* 26 Sept. 2018, www.salliemae.com/blog/becoming-resident-assistant-helped-pay-for-college/.

Burns, Melissa. "The College Puzzle A College Success Blog by Dr. Michael W. Kirst." *The College Puzzle,* 20 May 2017, collegepuzzle.stanford.edu/7-ways-to-save-money-on-food-in-college/.

"Cost." *Merriam-Webster,* Merriam-Webster, www.merriam-webster.com/dictionary/cost.

Fay, Bill. "Dining Costs Eating up College Students' Budget." *Debt.Org,* 9 Mar. 2018, www.debt.org/blog/dining-costs-eating-up-college-students-budget.

Federal Work-Study Jobs Help Students Earn Money to Pay for College or Career School. studentaid.gov/understand-aid/types/work-study. Accessed 2 July 2020.

Handel, Stephen. "Tips on Transferring from a 2-Year to a 4-Year College." *Tips on Transferring from a 2-Year to a 4-Year College,* www.bigfuture.collegeboard.org/find-colleges/college-101/tips-on-college-transferring-from-a-2-year-to-a-4-year-college.

Larsen, Linda. "NCES Report: About 80 Percent of College Students Change Major At least Once." *KIFI,* KIFI, 13 Oct. 2018, www.localnews8.com/news/education/nces-report-about-80-percent-of-college-students-change-major-at-least-once/806483499

"Subprime Education." *FAKE: Fake Money, Fake Teachers, Fake Assets: How Lies Are Making the Poor and Middle-Class Poorer,* by Robert T. Kiyosaki, Plata Publishing, 2019, pp. 153–153.

Mislinski, Jill. "The Fed's Financial Accounts: What Is Uncle Sam's Largest Asset?" *Advisorperspectives.com,* 12 June 2020. www.advisorperspectives.com/dshort/commentaries/2020/06/12/the-fed-s-financial-accounts-what-is-uncle-sam-s-largest-asset

Acknowledgement

I would like to thank Dr. Wilbur Brower who helped me with this project. Dr. Brower is the founder and president of W. Brower & Associates, a management consulting and training firm. I have known him for a long time, and he has always had a heart for the youth. He also helped me organize this book. Please check out his published books on www.amazon.com and his music on several platform streaming services.

Special thanks to Coastal Carolina Community College and Lees McRae College for giving me the chance to attend and pursue my future. Lastly, I would like to thank my father for not co-signing my college loan, which allowed me to find and create my own pathway to college. My father has been a positive example for me. He was the person that taught me the main principle of this book "How to Cut Cost." I remember my dad cutting cost for everything while I was growing up. He never bought a brand-new car he always tried to cut his cost for any and everything. Adopting my father's technique of cutting cost throughout my life has allowed me to obtain college degrees, buy cars, motorcycles, and a house at the fraction of the price. Maybe my next book will be called *"Chadwick's Father's Checklist."* Here in America there are many young men who are being guided through life without a father.

Below is a photo of my father and me together. My father once told me a quote: **"Son, sometimes what you don't know can hurt you!"** If you did not know how to cut the college costs, I hope you know much more now after reading this booklet.

About the Author

Charles Adam Chadwick Jr is a former college student who faced the challenge and obstacle of paying for his education alone. During his college experience, he unconsciously cut his college costs by thousands of dollars and obtained two degrees.

As many millennials struggle today to repay their student loans while hoping for government student loan forgiveness, Charles is not in that category. He was motivated to make it on his own by creating and taking advantage of every opportunity that came his way during college.

He has worked in many professions post-high school and college. He assisted his father in running the family plumbing business, worked as a cashier at Church's Chicken and Wal-Mart, as a Driver/Packer at a moving and storage business and delivered pizzas. In addition, he has worked as a Corrections Officer, Deputy Sheriff, Security Guard, Overseas Armed Guard, Unarmed Custody Officer, and a Construction Surveillance Technician Contractor. While many of these job fields may not be related directly to his degree in Communications, he has never been ashamed or afraid of hard work or opportunities.

Charles was born and raised in Jacksonville, NC, but he has resided in several countries outside the United States. He lists travel as an important factor in his life experiences, personal growth, and professional development.

www.ingramcontent.com/pod-product-compliance
Lightning Source LLC
Chambersburg PA
CBHW071038080526
44587CB00015B/2680